W9-AGM-428

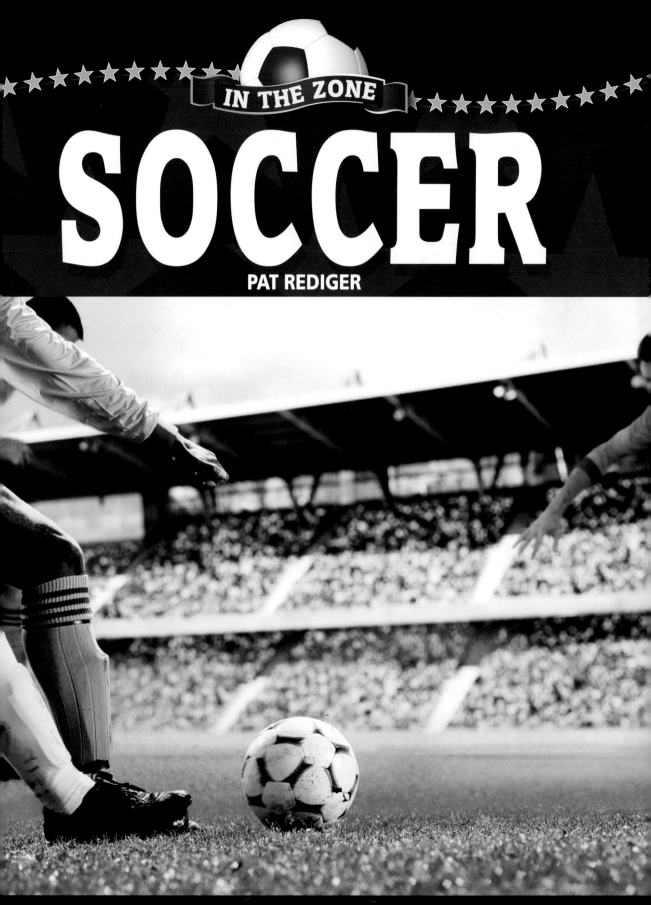

IN THE ZONE

SOCCER

PAT REDIGER

WEIGL PUBLISHERS INC.

Published by Weigl Publishers Inc.
350 5th Avenue, Suite 3304, PMB 6G
New York, NY 10118-0069

Website: www.weigl.com

Library of Congress Cataloging-in-Publication Data

Rediger, Pat, 1966-
 Soccer / Pat Rediger.
   p. cm. -- (In the Zone)
 Includes index.
 ISBN 978-1-60596-124-8 (hard cover : alk. paper) -- ISBN 978-1-60596-125-5 (soft cover : alk. paper)
 1. Soccer--Juvenile literature. I. Title.
 GV943.25.R43 2010
 796.334--dc22
                      2009008355

Printed in China
1 2 3 4 5 6 7 8 9 13 12 11 10 09

Weigl acknowledges Getty Images as its primary image supplier for this title.

Illustrations
Kenzie Browne: pages 9, 10 Left.

Heather C. Hudak Project Coordinator
Terry Paulhus Design
Kenzie Browne Layout

IN THE ZO

CONTENTS

What is **Soccer?**

Soccer players can kick a ball with a great deal of force.

It is believed that soccer began in China in 2500 BC. Back then, the ball was made of animal skins, and the players kicked it through a hole in a net. Soccer was played to celebrate the **emperor's** birthday. It was also played as a way to keep soldiers in shape.

■ Soccer has attracted enthusiastic fans since the early 1900s.

American Indians also played a similar game called *pascuckuakohowog*. This word means "they gather to play ball with the foot." They played on beaches, where the nets were about 1 mile (1.6 kilometers) apart. Sometimes, as many as 1,000 people played at a time. They could only tell their teammate by the paint and jewelry they wore. The games often lasted more than a day and ended with a feast.

The soccer game played today came from England, where it is called football. It is difficult to know exactly when people started playing the game there. New soccer rules were written in 1863, and they are the basis for what we play today.

Soccer is a great game because it can be played almost anywhere. All that is needed is a level patch of ground, a ball, and two teams. The players handle the ball mainly with their feet. To score, players kick the ball into the other team's net. The team with the most number of goals at the end of the game wins.

Soccer players do not need a great deal of equipment to start playing. All they really need is a ball, a pair of shoes, and comfortable clothing.

Many goalkeepers wear the number one on their jerseys. Their uniform is a different color from all the other players on their team.

Goalkeepers often wear pants, soft pads, gloves, and other protective equipment.

Players wear loose shorts. They are comfortable and do not get in the way of running or kicking the ball.

Players wear **cleats** to play soccer. These shoes have pieces of plastic on the bottoms for better grip. There are rules about the size and shape of the cleats on soccer shoes. If they are too long, they could hurt another player.

Players wear matching uniforms. They often have a large number on the back of their jerseys and a smaller one on the front.

There are hundreds of different kinds of soccer balls in use today. Soccer balls are round, made of leather, and bounce well. Balls must be 27 to 28 inches (69 to 71 centimeters) around. This is smaller than a basketball but larger than a volleyball. Soccer balls weigh between 14 and 16 ounces (397 and 454 grams).

During a soccer game, players may be asked to take off items that could hurt another player. These items include hard helmets, watches, or rings. Casts or braces must be wrapped so that no hard part of metal shows.

■ The same ball is used for the entire game unless the ball is defective.

Players often wear shin pads to protect their legs.

■ There is a goalpost at each end of the playing field.

The Playing Field

A soccer field, which is also called a pitch, can vary in size, but it is always rectangular. It can be no more than 130 yards by 100 yards (119 by 91 meters).

The goalposts are 8 yards (7 m) wide and 8 feet (2.4 m) high. The **crossbars** around the goal are usually made of wood or metal. The goal area itself is 20 yards by 6 yards (18 by 5.5 m). Goal kicks are taken from anywhere in this area. The **penalty** area is in front of each goal. Only the goalkeeper is allowed to use his or her hands here.

The corner flags sit on posts. They are at least 5 feet (1.5 m) high and are placed in each corner. Flags are also placed halfway down the field on both sides. The corner area extends out from the corner flag. The ball is placed here for a corner kick.

The center circle is 10 yards (9 m) in **radius**. This circle keeps one team away from the ball when the other team takes the **kickoff**.

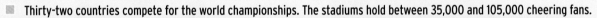

Thirty-two countries compete for the world championships. The stadiums hold between 35,000 and 105,000 cheering fans.

Sports Venues

To learn more about soccer fields, go to
www.sportsknowhow.com/soccer/
dimensions/soccer-dimensions.html.

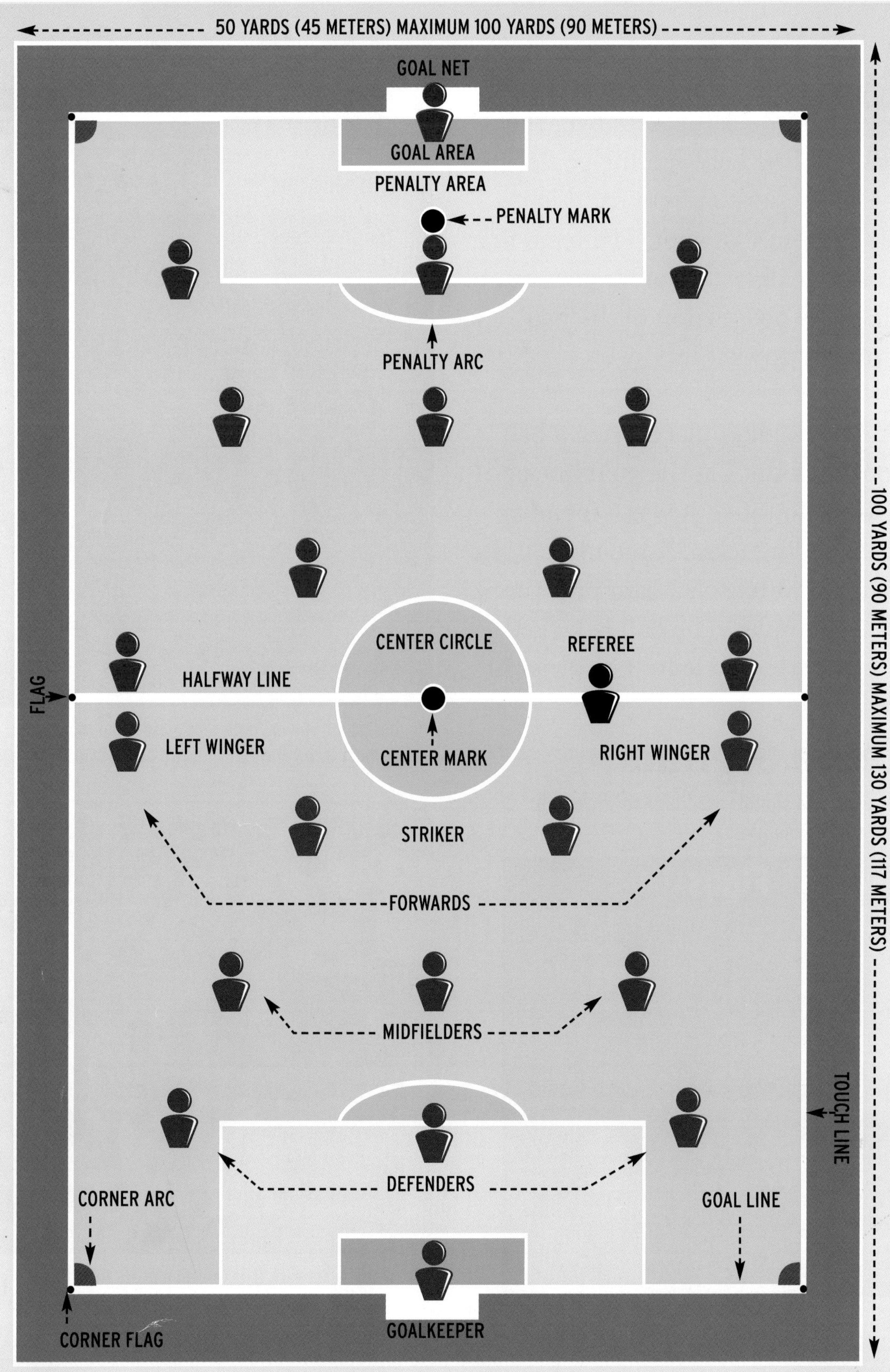

50 YARDS (45 METERS) MAXIMUM 100 YARDS (90 METERS)

100 YARDS (90 METERS) MAXIMUM 130 YARDS (117 METERS)

GOAL NET

GOAL AREA

PENALTY AREA

PENALTY MARK

PENALTY ARC

CENTER CIRCLE

REFEREE

FLAG

HALFWAY LINE

LEFT WINGER

CENTER MARK

RIGHT WINGER

STRIKER

FORWARDS

MIDFIELDERS

TOUCH LINE

CORNER ARC

DEFENDERS

GOAL LINE

CORNER FLAG

GOALKEEPER

9

A soccer match lasts two periods of 45 minutes. A goal is scored when the ball passes over the **goal line** between the goalposts. If the ball goes out of bounds, it is thrown in from that spot. The team that touches the ball last before it goes out of bounds loses **possession** of the ball. The other team throws it in.

A corner kick takes place when a ball goes out of bounds at the goal line and the last one to touch it was a member of the defending team. A member of the **attacking**, or offensive, team puts the ball back into play. The ball is kicked from the quarter circle in the corner of the field.

During a throw-in, both feet must be on the ground. The player must throw the ball with two hands over his or her head.

Referee Signals

Referees use hand signals and flags to show calls. These are some examples.

Flags

GOAL	SEND OFF FIELD
THROW IN	CORNER KICK

When a free kick is taken, all players from the opposing team must stand 10 yards (9 m) away. The opposing team can move toward the ball after it is kicked.

A goal kick occurs after the ball passes over the goal line and the last one to touch it was a member of the attacking team. A member of the defending team puts the ball back into play. The ball is kicked from inside the goal area. It must pass outside the penalty area before another player can touch it.

It is against the rules to kick or trip another player. Players also cannot hold or push other players. The ball cannot be handled with the player's hands or arms. Goalkeepers, however, can use their hands to block shots.

Players are allowed to use their bodies against the player with the ball, but they cannot push or hold on to other players on the field.

If these rules are broken, the ball is handed over to the other team. If the rules are broken again and again, the referee can penalize the player or the team. The referee can stop the game at any time if a **foul** has occurred. The referee may award the other team a penalty kick if a player breaks the rules. His or her decisions are final.

The linespeople help the referee. They determine when the ball is out of play. They also show which side can take a corner kick, goal kick, or throw-in.

Goalkeepers do not have much time to react to a shot. Sometimes, they just have to guess whether a player will shoot to the right or left side of the net.

Sports Rules

To read more about soccer rules, visit www.soccerrules.org.

Positions

There are several positions on a soccer team. The goalkeeper's job is to block the other team's shots on the net. Goalkeepers can use their hands to move the ball only inside the penalty area. If they leave this area, they are treated like any other player and must use their feet to move the ball.

Defenders help their goalkeeper stop the other team from scoring. It is their job to prevent the other team's players from shooting at the goal at all. Defenders help block shots and get the ball away from the other team.

Different types of defenders play in different parts of the field. Fullbacks play down the sides. Centers play mainly in the area in front of the goal. Sometimes, a team will have sweepers who go where they are most needed.

Any player on the team can substitute for the goalkeeper as long as the referee is informed.

Soccer games are usually low-scoring. Scoring just one goal can be the difference between a win or a loss.

Midfielders move the ball mainly from the defenders to the forwards. Their job is to gain control of the ball when it is in the middle of the field. When the other team has the ball, midfielders try to get it back. When their own team has the ball, they try to set up plays to help the team score.

Teams usually have between two and five midfielders. A flank midfield player plays down the sides of the field. A central midfield player tries to score when attacking and tries to prevent a goal when defending.

Attackers, or forwards, try to score goals. Teams use one to four players in this position. They must be able to pass well and control the ball. Attackers can kick the ball hard and right on target.

■ Soccer players sometimes hit the ball with their head instead of their feet.

■ Defenders are sometimes called fullbacks. They take the ball from the other team and pass it to their teammates so they can score.

Leagues

Most children begin playing soccer in local leagues. This is where they learn how to play the sport. Those players who work hard can eventually play for college or university teams or the national teams. There are six men's national teams: World Cup, indoor, university, Olympic, and under 17 years old. There are two women's national teams: World Cup/Olympic and under 20 years old.

World Cup soccer is a great event to watch. Each country fields its best players in hopes of winning the cup.

FIFA Club World Cup Japan 2008 presented by TOY

The World Cup takes place every four years.

The best players from universities and high schools are chosen to play for the national teams. They compete against players from other countries. The biggest tournament for national teams is the World Cup. The first World Cup tournament was held in 1930. Every country in the world that plays soccer competes in this tournament.

Those who compete for the national teams are not paid. There are leagues for players who want to earn money. For example, Major League Soccer has 12 professional teams playing throughout the United States.

School teams are an excellent place to learn from experienced players and coaches.

Winning any competition is a major accomplishment.

Superstars of the Sport

Soccer has had many fantastic players in its history. Many of these have made children want to play the game, too.

Bobby Charlton

TEAM: Manchester United

CAREER FACTS:
- Bobby played forward for Manchester for twenty years. Upon his retirement, Bobby had scored 245 goals and only had one foul for delaying a free kick.
- In 1966, Bobby was voted the soccer player of the year.
- In 1958, Bobby survived a plane crash that killed 23 people, including eight soccer players.
- In 1994, Bobby was knighted for his services as an ambassador to soccer.
- Bobby led Manchester United to many victories, including the World Cup and the European Cup.

Pele

TEAM: Brazilian National Team

CAREER FACTS:
- Pele's first job was shining shoes.
- At the age of 15, Pele was invited to play for the Santos Futebol Club in Sao Paulo.
- When Pele was 16, he joined the Brazilian National Team.
- In his career, Pele played in 14 World Cups and scored 12 goals in those competitions.
- In 1971, Pele joined the New York Cosmos to help make the game more popular in North America.

Paolo Maldini

TEAM: AC Milan

CAREER FACTS:
- Paolo's father was a great soccer player and was captain of the AC Milan team in Italy.
- Paolo played several different positions in school before becoming a defender.
- Paolo played his first game for AC Milan in 1985. He was only sixteen years old.
- In 1988, Paolo was named to the Italian National Team.
- In 1994, Paolo became the captain of the Italian team and was named World Soccer's Player of the Year.
- Paolo became captain of AC Milan in 1998.

Mia Hamm

TEAM: United States National Soccer Team

CAREER FACTS:
- At fifteen years old, Mia was the youngest player to play with the United States National Soccer Team.
- In 1995 and 1997, Mia was named the Women's World Cup Most Valuable Player.
- Mia was named U.S. Soccer's Female Athlete of the Year from 1994 to 1998.
- Mia established a foundation to raise money for bone marrow research. Her brother had died of a rare blood disorder and had trouble receiving a bone marrow transplant.

Sports Stars

To read more about soccer players, go to http://expert football.com/players.

The stars of today are thrilling fans and attracting more attention to soccer.

Landon Donovan

TEAM: F.C. Bayern Munich

CAREER FACTS:

- Donovan joined his first competitive league at the age of five. Even though most of his competitors were older, he scored seven goals in his first game with the league.
- In 2003, Donovan was named the U.S. Soccer Athlete of the Year.
- He is the only player to win the Honda Player of the Year Award five times. No other player has won the award more than twice.
- Donovan is the all-time leading scorer for the United States.

Dwight Yorke

TEAM: Sunderland A.F.C.

CAREER FACTS:

- Dwight joined his high school soccer team. The national team coach spotted him and invited him to play in a game against England.
- In 1989, Dwight joined the Aston Villa team in Birmingham, England. He became the club's top scorer and led them to many successes.
- After nine years, Dwight was signed by Manchester United. Dwight led United in scoring and was named the top player in the league.
- Dwight is loved in his home country of Trinidad and Tobago. A song has been written about him called "The Duke of Manchester."
- Dwight has a stadium named after him in Bacolot, Tobago. It is called The Dwight Yorke Stadium. He was also named the Sports Ambassador for his country after the 2006 FIFA World Cup.

Ronaldo Luiz Nazario de Lima

TEAM: S.C. Corinthians Paulista

CAREER FACTS:

- Ronaldo was part of the Brazilian teams that won the 1994 and 2002 World Cups. He is the highest goal scorer in the history of the World Cup, with 15 goals.
- Since 2005, Ronaldo has been the co-owner of A1 Team Brazil.
- He is known for being a high scorer. When he played for Cruzeiro Esporte Clube at the age of 18, he scored 12 goals in 13 games.
- Ronaldo has served as a peace ambassador for the United Nations.

Kasey Keller

TEAM: Seattle Sounders FC

CAREER FACTS:

- In 1994, Kasey played for Leicester, a top European team.
- Kasey started in more than 300 professional games in Europe. This is more than twice as many as any other American player.
- Kasey led the United States National Team to win the 1998 Gold Cup against Brazil.
- Kasey was the starting goalkeeper for the United States World Cup team in 1998.
- Kasey is one of the world's best goalkeepers and the U.S.A.'s leader in wins.

Staying Healthy

Just like you cannot run a car without fuel, you cannot play a good game of soccer without healthy food. Good **nutrition** is the key to keeping players at the top of their game.

Players often eat a variety of **carbohydrates** before they play. This means eating bread, raisins, watermelon, carrots, most types of cereals, spaghetti, bananas, and pineapple. They provide extra fuel for muscles during the game. These foods give players more energy on the field. A balanced diet of the major food groups is also important.

■ Drinking plenty of water every day also helps keep people running well.

■ Fruits and vegetables, along with breads and cereals, milk products, and meats, help keep people healthy.

There are many ways to train to become a better soccer player. Soccer players are always on the run, so they need to have strong hearts as well as muscles. Players often practice running while controlling the ball with their feet. They also practice running backwards without crashing into other players. Leg strength is important, and jumping, lunging, and stretching exercises help make players' leg muscles stronger.

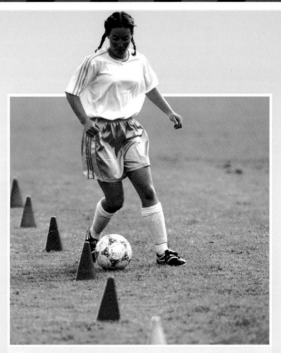

During practice, players work on controlling the ball to help improve their skills.

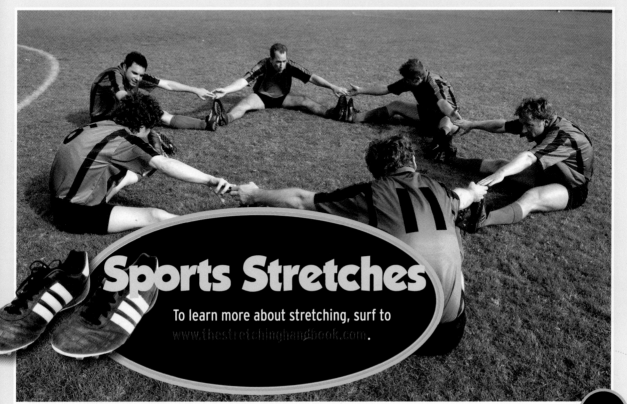

Sports Stretches

To learn more about stretching, surf to www.thestretchinghandbook.com.

Stretching before and after a game helps prevent injury.

Soccer Brain Teasers

Do you think you know all you need to know about soccer? See if you can answers these questions about this exciting sport!

Q When did people first begin playing soccer?

A It is believed that soccer began in China in 2500 BC.

Q What size are the goalposts?

A The goalposts are 8 yards (7 m) wide and 8 feet (2.4 m) high.

Q Who was the youngest player to play with the United States Women's National Soccer Team?

A At fifteen years old, Mia Hamm was the youngest player to play with the United States Women's National Soccer Team.

Q When does a corner kick take place?

A A corner kick takes place when a ball goes out of bounds at the goal line and the last one to touch it was a member of the defending team.

Q When was the first World Cup tournament?

A The first World Cup tournament was held in 1930.

Q How many midfielders are on a soccer team?

A Teams usually have between two and five midfielders.

Glossary

attacking: an offensive move; having the ball and trying to score goals

carbohydrates: foods that have materials that are good for building muscles and providing energy

cleats: shoes with hard plastic on the bottoms; they help players get a better grip on the grass when they run

crossbars: the three poles that make up the goal

emperor: the ruler of an empire

foul: a referee call when a player breaks one of the rules

goal line: the line across the field that acts as the boundary

kickoff: a kick that puts a ball into play from the center line at the start of a quarter or after a goal has been scored

nutrition: foods that make up a good diet

penalty: punishment for breaking a rule or law

possession: having control of the ball; it changes from team to team many times throughout a game

radius: a straight line out from the center of a circle that reaches to the edge

Index